PLAY ANY OF THESE
ROCK HITS
ONLY FIVE C

WISE PUBLICATIONS
part of The Music Sales Group
London / New York / Paris / Sydney / Copenhagen / Berlin / Madrid / Hong Kong / Tokyo

Published by
Wise Publications
14-15 Berners Street,
London W1T 3LJ, UK.

Exclusive Distributors:
Music Sales Limited
Distribution Centre, Newmarket Road,
Bury St Edmunds, Suffolk IP33 3YB, UK.
Music Sales Pty Limited
20 Resolution Drive, Caringbah,
NSW 2229, Australia.

Order No. AM1003783
ISBN: 978-1-78038-197-8
This book © Copyright 2011 Wise Publications,
a division of Music Sales Limited.

Edited by Adrian Hopkins.
Printed in the EU.

Your Guarantee of Quality
As publishers, we strive to produce every book
to the highest commercial standards.

This book has been carefully designed to minimise
awkward page turns and to make playing from it a real pleasure.

Particular care has been given to specifying acid-free,
neutral-sized paper made from pulps which have not been
elemental chlorine bleached. This pulp is from farmed
sustainable forests and was produced with special
regard for the environment.

Throughout, the printing and binding have been planned
to ensure a sturdy, attractive publication which should
give years of enjoyment.

If your copy fails to meet our high standards,
please inform us and we will gladly replace it.

www.musicsales.com

Are You Gonna Be My Girl

Words & Music by
Nic Cester & Cameron Muncey

Intro

	: A	A	A	A	
A	A	A	A	:	*Bass only*
A	A	A	A	
Go!
A	A	A	A	|| *Guitar*

Verse 1

       A N.C.
Said 1, 2, 3, take my hand and come with me,

Because you look so fine,

                A
That I really wanna make you mine.

       N.C.
I say you look so fine,

                A
That I really wanna make you mine.

      N.C.
Oh, 4, 5, 6 c'mon and get your kicks,

Now you don't need money,

              A
When you look like that, do ya honey?

Bridge 1

D   **C** **G**
    Big black boots,

D   **C** **G**
    Long brown hair,

D
    She's so sweet,

C **G** **D**
With her   get back stare.

Chorus 1

A
Well I could see,

C
You home with me,

D   **A**
But you were with another man, yeah!

                                    C
I know we ain't got   much to say,

D   **A**
Before I let you get a - way, yeah!

| **E** | **E** | **G** | **G**   ‖

N.C.
I said, are you gonna be my girl?

Link | **A** | **A** | **A** | **A** |

              | **A** | **A** | **A** | **A**   ‖

                              A N.C.
Verse 2   Well, it's a 1, 2, 3, take my hand and come with me,

Because you look so fine,

                                          D
That I really wanna make you mine.

                    N.C.
I say you look so fine,

                                          D
That I really wanna make you mine.

              N.C.
Oh, 4, 5, 6 c'mon and get your kicks,

Now you don't need money,

                                    D
With a face like that, do ya?

Bridge 2   As Bridge 1

Chorus 2   As Chorus 1

Link | A | A | A | A |

| A | A | A | A   ‖

Guitar solo | A   A | A | C | C | D   D | A | A   ‖
Oh yeah.   Oh   yeah.
| A | A | C | C | D   D | A | A   ‖
C'mon!

Chorus 3
A
I could see,
C
You home with me,
D   **A**
But you were with another man, yeah!

I know we ain't got **C** much to say,
D   **A**
Before I let you get a - way, yeah!

Uh, be my girl.
C
Be my girl.
D   **A**   **G D**
Are you gonna be my girl,   yeah?

Baba O'Riley

Words & Music by
Pete Townshend

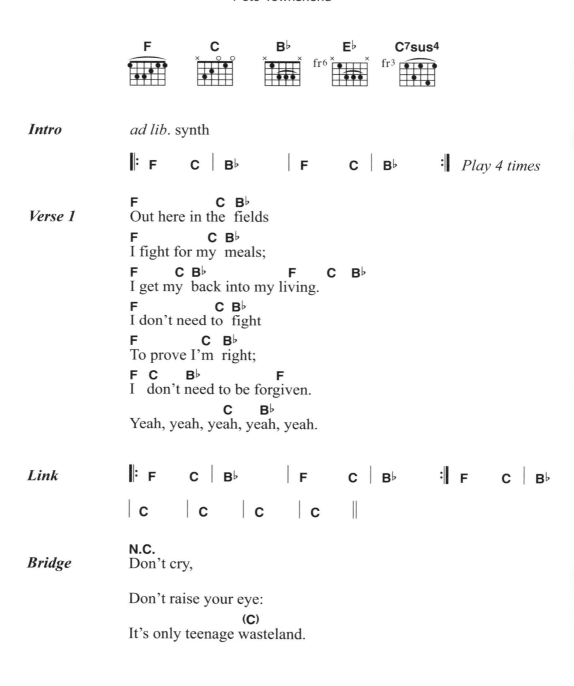

Intro

ad lib. synth

‖: F   C | B♭ | F   C | B♭   :‖ *Play 4 times*

Verse 1

F   C B♭
Out here in the fields

F   C B♭
I fight for my meals;

F   C B♭   F C B♭
I get my back into my living.

F   C B♭
I don't need to fight

F   C B♭
To prove I'm right;

F C   B♭   F
I don't need to be forgiven.

                 C   B♭
Yeah, yeah, yeah, yeah, yeah.

Link

‖: F   C | B♭ | F   C | B♭   :‖ F   C | B♭

| C | C | C | C   ‖

Bridge

N.C.
Don't cry,

Don't raise your eye:

               (C)
It's only teenage wasteland.

Verse 2

F   C B♭
Sally, take my hand,

F   C B♭
We'll travel south 'cross land

F   C
Put out the fire

       B♭   F   C B♭
And don't look past my shoulder.

F   C B♭
The exodus is   here,

F   C B♭
The happy ones are near,

F   C
Let's get together

       B♭   F   C B♭
Before we get much older.

Solo | F   C | B♭   C | F   C | B♭ ||

Chorus

               F   C B♭
Teenage wasteland,

                    C   F   C B♭
It's only teenage wasteland.

         C   F
Teenage wasteland

C   B♭
Oh yeah,

         C   F   C B♭
Teenage wasteland.

               C   B♭
They're all wasted!

Solo 2 ||: C | B♭ | F | E♭   :||

                | F | F | E♭ | E♭ ||

Violin solo | F   (*ad lib*. for 36 bars) ||

Outro | C⁷sus⁴ | C⁷sus⁴ | C⁷sus⁴ | C⁷sus⁴ | F ||

Danger! High Voltage

Words & Music by
Tyler Spencer, Joseph Frezza, Stephen Nawara, Anthony Selph & Cory Martin

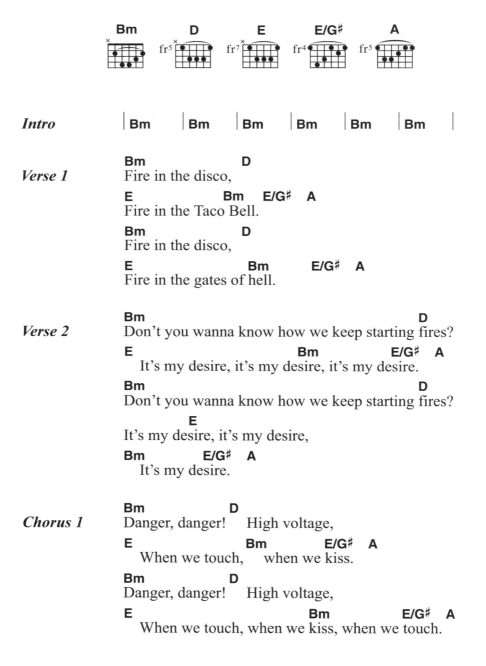

Intro | Bm | Bm | Bm | Bm | Bm | Bm |

Verse 1

Bm   D
Fire in the disco,
E   Bm E/G♯ A
Fire in the Taco Bell.
Bm   D
Fire in the disco,
E   Bm E/G♯ A
Fire in the gates of hell.

Verse 2

Bm   D
Don't you wanna know how we keep starting fires?
E   Bm E/G♯ A
It's my desire, it's my desire, it's my desire.
Bm   D
Don't you wanna know how we keep starting fires?
E
It's my desire, it's my desire,
Bm E/G♯ A
It's my desire.

Chorus 1

Bm   D
Danger, danger! High voltage,
E   Bm E/G♯ A
When we touch, when we kiss.
Bm   D
Danger, danger! High voltage,
E   Bm   E/G♯ A
When we touch, when we kiss, when we touch.

Chorus 2

Bm   D
Danger, danger!   High voltage,

E   Bm   E/G♯   A
  When we touch,   when we kiss.

Bm   D
Danger, danger!   High voltage,

E   Bm
  When we touch, when we kiss,

      E/G♯   A
When we touch, when we (kiss).

Guitar Solo

‖: Bm | D | E | Bm E/G♯ A :‖ *Play 4 times*
  kiss.

Verse 3

      Bm   D
Well don't you wanna know how we keep starting fires?

E   Bm   E/G♯   A
  It's my desire,   it's my desire.

Bm   D
Don't you wanna know how we keep starting fires?

E   Bm   E/G♯   A
  It's my desire,   it's my desire.

Chorus 3   As Chorus 1

Chorus 4   As Chorus 1

Sax Solo

‖: Bm |D |E |Bm E/G♯ A :‖

Verse 4

Bm
Fire in the disco,

D
Fire in the disco,

E   Bm   E/G♯ A
Fire in the Taco Bell.

Bm   D
Fire in the disco,

D
Fire in the disco,

E   Bm   E/G♯ A
Fire in the gates of hell.

Outro

| Bm |D |E |Bm E/G♯ A |
               The gates of hell.

‖: Bm |D |E |Bm E/G♯ A :‖
                           Repeat to fade

Do Wah Diddy Diddy

Words & Music by
Jeff Barry & Ellie Greenwich

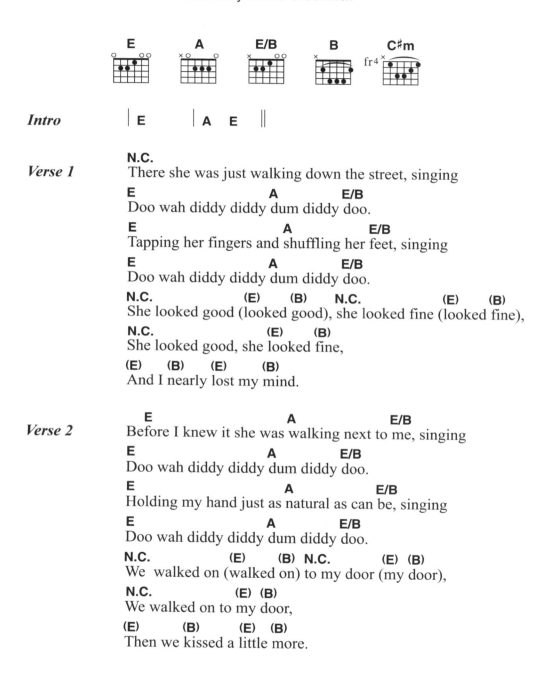

Intro | E | A E ‖

Verse 1

N.C.
There she was just walking down the street, singing
E   A   E/B
Doo wah diddy diddy dum diddy doo.
E   A   E/B
Tapping her fingers and shuffling her feet, singing
E   A   E/B
Doo wah diddy diddy dum diddy doo.
N.C.   (E)   (B)   N.C.   (E)   (B)
She looked good (looked good), she looked fine (looked fine),
N.C.   (E)   (B)
She looked good, she looked fine,
(E)   (B)   (E)   (B)
And I nearly lost my mind.

Verse 2

E   A   E/B
Before I knew it she was walking next to me, singing
E   A   E/B
Doo wah diddy diddy dum diddy doo.
E   A   E/B
Holding my hand just as natural as can be, singing
E   A   E/B
Doo wah diddy diddy dum diddy doo.
N.C.   (E)   (B) N.C.   (E) (B)
We walked on (walked on) to my door (my door),
N.C.   (E) (B)
We walked on to my door,
(E)   (B)   (E) (B)
Then we kissed a little more.

Bridge 1

   E   C♯m
   Whoa, I knew we was falling in love,

A   B
   Yes I did, and so I told her all the things I'd been dreaming of.

Verse 3

         E   A   E/B
Now we're together nearly every single day, singing

E   A   E/B
Doo wah diddy diddy dum diddy doo.

E   A   E/B
We're so happy and that's how we're gonna stay, singing

E   A   E/B
Doo wah diddy diddy dum diddy doo.

N.C.   (E) (B) N.C.   (E) (B)
Well, I'm hers (I'm hers), she's mine (she's mine),

N.C   (E) (B)
I'm hers, she's mine,

(E)   (B)   (E)   (B)
Wedding bells are gonna chime.

Bridge 2

   E   C♯m
   Whoa, I knew we was falling in love,

A   B
   Yes I did, and so I told her all the things I'd been dreaming of.

Verse 4

         N.C.
Now we're together nearly every single day, singing

E   A   E/B
Doo wah diddy diddy dum diddy doo.

E   A   E/B
We're so happy and that's how we're gonna stay, singing

E   A   E/B
Doo wah diddy diddy dum diddy doo.

N.C.   (E) (B) N.C.   (E) (B)
Well I'm hers (I'm hers), she's mine (she's mine),

N.C.   (E) (B)
I'm hers, she's mine,

(E)   (B)   (E)   (B)
Wedding bells are gonna chime.

| B | B | ‖

Coda

‖: E   A   E/B
  Doo wah diddy diddy dum diddy doo. :‖ *Play 3 times*

Don't Stop

Words & Music by
Christine McVie

E   A/E   D   A   B

Intro

‖: E A/E | E A/E | E A/E | E A/E :‖

Verse 1

E   D   A
If you wake up and don't want to smile,
E   D   A
If it takes just a little while,
E   D   A
Open your eyes, look at the day,
B
You'll see things in a different way.

Chorus 1

E   D   A
Don't stop thinking about tomorrow,
E   D   A
Don't stop, it'll soon be here.
E   D   A
It'll be better than before,
B
Yesterday's gone, yesterday's gone.

Link 1

| E D | A | E D | A   ‖

Verse 2

E   D   A
Why not think about times to come,
E   D   A
And not about the things that you've done?
E   D   A
If your life was bad for you,
B
Just think what tomorrow will do.

Chorus 2   As Chorus 1

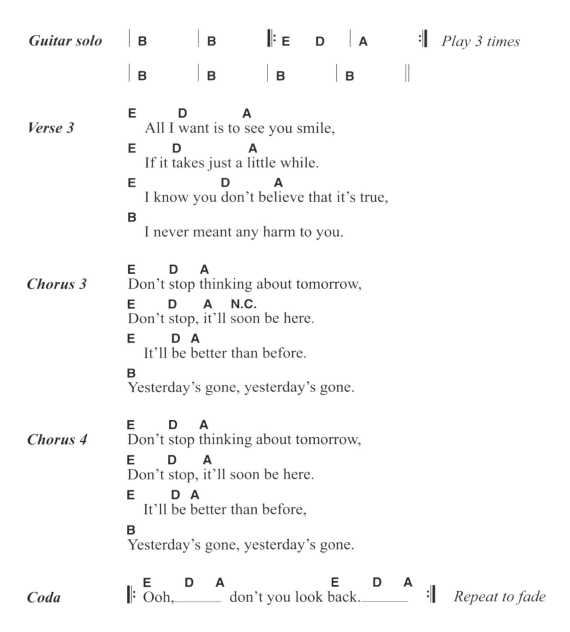

Guitar solo | B | B   ‖: E   D | A   :‖ *Play 3 times*

| B | B | B | B   ‖

Verse 3
E   D   A
All I want is to see you smile,
E   D   A
If it takes just a little while.
E   D   A
I know you don't believe that it's true,
B
I never meant any harm to you.

Chorus 3
E   D   A
Don't stop thinking about tomorrow,
E   D   A   N.C.
Don't stop, it'll soon be here.
E   D A
It'll be better than before.
B
Yesterday's gone, yesterday's gone.

Chorus 4
E   D   A
Don't stop thinking about tomorrow,
E   D   A
Don't stop, it'll soon be here.
E   D A
It'll be better than before,
B
Yesterday's gone, yesterday's gone.

Coda   ‖: E   D   A   E   D   A   :‖ *Repeat to fade*
Ooh,_____ don't you look back._____

13

I Can't Explain

Words & Music by
Words & Music by Pete Townshend

E   D   A   B   C#m   fr4

Intro

| E D | A E | E D | A E | E D | A E ||

Verse 1

           E   D   A   E
Got a feeling inside, (can't explain,)
               D   A   E
It's a certain kind, (can't explain.)
                  D   A   E
I feel hot and cold, (can't explain,)
                    D   B   E   E D
Yeah, down in my soul, yeah, (can't explain.)
     A   E
I said, can't explain
                  D
I'm feelin' good now, yeah,
        A   E
But can't explain.

Verse 2

      E   D   A   E
Dizzy in the head and I'm feelin' blue,
               D   A   E
The things you said, well maybe they're true.
             D   A   E
Gettin' funny dreams again and again,
             D   B
I know what it means but…

Bridge 1

     E
Can't explain,
      C#m   A
I think it's love, try to say it to you,
        B   E   D   A   E
When I feel blue, but I can't explain. (Can't explain.)
                  D   A   E
Yeah, hear what I'm sayin' girl. (Can't explain.)

Solo | E   D | A   E | E   D | A   E ||

Verse 3
E   D   A   E
Dizzy in the head and I'm feelin' bad,
                     D   A   E
Things you said have got me real mad.
                         D   A   E
I'm gettin' funny dreams again and again,
                      D   B
I know what it means but…

Bridge 2
E
Can't explain,
  C♯m   A
I think it's love, try to say it to you,
         B   E   D   A   E
When I feel blue, but I can't explain. (Can't explain.)
                     D   A   E
Yeah, just hear me one more time now. (Can't explain.)

Solo ||: E   D | A   E | E   D | A   E   :||

E   D   A   E
(Ooh, ooh.) I said I can't explain, yeah,
           D   A   E
(Ooh, ooh.) You drive me out of my mind.
           D   A   E
(Ooh, ooh.) Yeah, I'm the worryin' kind, yeah,
           D   A   E
(Ooh, ooh.) I said I can't explain.

The Jean Genie

Words & Music by
David Bowie

E   A   B   Dsus4   D

Intro | E | E | E   A | E   A | E   A | E   A ||

Verse 1
       E   A   E   A
    A small Jean Genie   snuck off to the city
E   A   E   A
Strung out on lasers   and   slash-back blazers,
        E   A   E   A
And ate all your razors   while pulling the waiters.
E   A   E   A
Talking 'bout Monroe   and walking on Snow White,
E   A   E   A
New York's a go-go   and everything tastes nice.
       E   A
    Poor little Greenie.

Link 1 | E   A | E   A | E | B ||

Chorus 1
B
    The Jean Genie lives on his back,

The Jean Genie loves chimney stacks.

He's outrageous, he screams and he bawls,

Jean Genie let yourself go!

Link 2 | A | A Dsus4 D | A | A Dsus4 D |

| E   A | E   A | E   A | E   A ||

Verse 2
       E   A   E   A
Sits like a man but he smiles like a reptile,
        E   A   E   A
She love him, she love him but just for a short while
        E   A   E
She'll scratch in the sand, won't let go his hand;
A E   A E   A
He says he's a beautician and sells you nutrition,

cont.

        E   A E   A
And keeps all your dead hair   for   making up underwear.
   E   A
     Poor little Greenie.

Link 3 | E   A | E   A | E ||

Chorus 2   As Chorus 1

Link 4 | A | A Dsus⁴ D | A | A Dsus⁴ D |

           | E   A | E   A | E   A | E   A ||

Bridge

        E   A E   A
He's so simple minded he can't drive his module,
      E   A E   A E
He bites on the neon and sleeps in a capsule.
A E   A E A E
  Loves to be loved,   loves to be loved.

Guitar solo ‖: E   A | E   A | E   A | E   A :‖ *Play 3 times*

             | E | E ||

Chorus 3   As Chorus 1

Link 5 | A | A Dsus⁴ D | A | A Dsus⁴ D ||
                       (go!)   (go!)

Chorus 4   As Chorus 1

Link 6 | A | A Dsus⁴ D | A | A Dsus⁴ D |
                       (go!)   (go!)

           | E   A | E   A | E   A | E   A ||

Coda   ‖: E   A | E   A | E   A | E   A :‖

           | E | E | E | E |

           | E | E | E ||

Like A Rolling Stone

Words & Music by
Bob Dylan

C   F   Dm   Em   G

Intro | C   F | C   F | C   F | C   F ||

Verse 1

```
C                        Dm
Once upon a time you dressed so fine
        Em                      F          G
You threw the bums a dime in your prime,   didn't you?
C             Dm                    Em
People'd call, say, "Beware doll, you're bound to fall"
                  F           G
You thought they were all    kiddin' you
F            G
    You used to   laugh about
F                    G
    Everybody that was   hangin' out
F          Em   Dm            C
    Now you don't talk so loud
F             Em   Dm              C
    Now you don't seem so proud
Dm                           F          G
About having to be scrounging   your next meal
```

Chorus 1

```
                C   F G
How does it feel
                C   F G
How does it feel
                    C   F G
To be without a home
                    C   F G
Like a complete unknown
                    C   F G
Like a rolling stone?
```

Link 1 | C   F | G | G ||

Verse 2

           C   Dm   Em
You've gone to the finest school alright, Miss Lonely

            F   G
But you know you only used to get juiced in it

         C   Dm   Em
And nobody has ever taught you how to live out on the street

                      F   G
And now you find out you're gonna have to get used to it

F   G
  You said you'd never compromise

F   G
  With the mystery tramp, but now you realize

F   Em   Dm C
  He's not selling any alibis

F   Em   Dm   C
As you stare into the vacuum of his eyes

      Dm   F   G
And ask him do you want to make a deal?"

Chorus 2

          C   F G
How does it feel

          C   F G
How does it feel

            C   F G
To be on your own

               C   F G
With no direction home

            C   F G
A complete unknown

           C   F G
Like a rolling stone?

Link 2 | C   F | G | G ||

Verse 3

        C   Dm
You never turned around to see the frowns

 Em   F
  On the jugglers and the clowns

                      G
When they all come down and did tricks for you

      C   Dm
You never understood that it ain't no good

  Em   F   G
You shouldn't let other people get your kicks for you

cont.

F   G

You used to ride on the chrome horse with your   diplomat

F   G

Who carried on his shoulder a   Siamese cat

F   Em   Dm   C

Ain't it hard   when you discover that

F   Em   Dm   C

He really wasn't where it's at

Dm   F   G

After he took from you everything he could steal?

Chorus 3

                  C   F G

How does it feel

                  C   F G

How does it feel

                     C   F G

To be on your own

                         C   F G

With no direction home

                            C   F G

Like a complete unknown

                     C   F G

Like a rolling stone?

Link 3

| C   F | G | G   ‖

Verse 4

C   Dm   Em

Princess on the steeple and all the   pretty people

             F   G

They're drinkin', thinkin' that they   got it made

C   Dm

Exchanging all kinds of precious gifts

Em   F

But you'd better lift your diamond ring,

G

You'd better pawn it babe

F   G

You used to be   so amused

F   G

At Napoleon in rags   and the language that he used

```
            F                   Em                    Dm      C
cont.         Go to him now, he calls you, you can't refuse
            F                   Em                 Dm          C
              When you got nothing, you got   nothing to lose
            Dm                                   F          G
              You're invisible now, you got no secrets to conceal


                                 C     F   G
Chorus 4      How does it feel
                                 C    F   G
              How does it feel
                                   C      F   G
              To be on your own
                                    C      F   G
              With no direction home
                                     C      F   G
              Like a complete unknown
                                   C     F   G
              Like a rolling stone?


Coda         ‖: C    F   │ G        │ C    F    │ G        :‖   Repeat to fade
```

Little Deuce Coupe

Words & Music by
Brian Wilson & Roger Christian

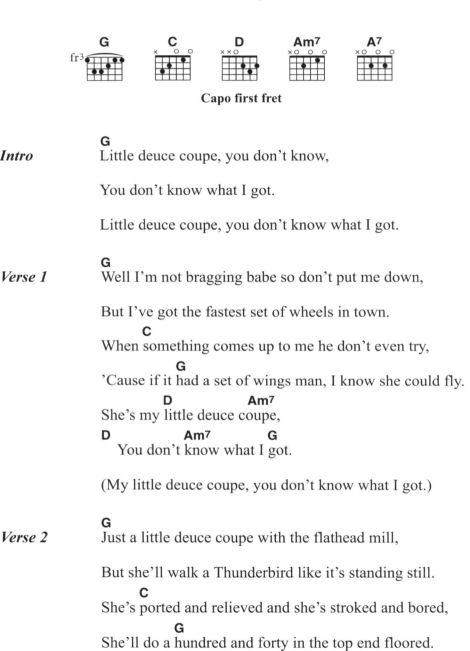

G C D Am7 A7

fr3

Capo first fret

Intro

G
Little deuce coupe, you don't know,

You don't know what I got.

Little deuce coupe, you don't know what I got.

Verse 1

G
Well I'm not bragging babe so don't put me down,

But I've got the fastest set of wheels in town.
   C
When something comes up to me he don't even try,
    G
'Cause if it had a set of wings man, I know she could fly.
   D   Am7
She's my little deuce coupe,
D   Am7   G
 You don't know what I got.

(My little deuce coupe, you don't know what I got.)

Verse 2

G
Just a little deuce coupe with the flathead mill,

But she'll walk a Thunderbird like it's standing still.
   C
She's ported and relieved and she's stroked and bored,
    G
She'll do a hundred and forty in the top end floored.

cont.

          D   **Am7**
She's my little deuce coupe,

D   **Am7**   **G**
  You don't know what I got.

(My little deuce coupe, you don't know what I got.)

Bridge

G   **C**
She's got a competition clutch with the four on the floor,

         G
And she purrs like a kitten till the lake pipes roar.

     C
And if that ain't enough to make you flip your lid,

      A7   **D**
There's one more thing, I got the pink slip, daddy.

Verse 3

       G
And coming off the line when the light turns green,

Well she blows 'em outta the water like you never seen.

     C
I get pushed out of shape and it's hard to steer,

    G
When I get rubber in all four gears.

          D   **Am7**
She's my little deuce coupe,

D   **Am7**   **G**
  You don't know what I got.

(My little deuce coupe, you don't know what I got.)

          D   **Am7**
She's my little deuce coupe,

D   **Am7**   **G**
  You don't know what I got.

(My little deuce coupe, you don't know what I got.)

          D   **Am7**
She's my little deuce coupe,

D   **Am7**   **G**
  You don't know what I got.   *To fade*

Metal Guru

Words & Music by
Marc Bolan

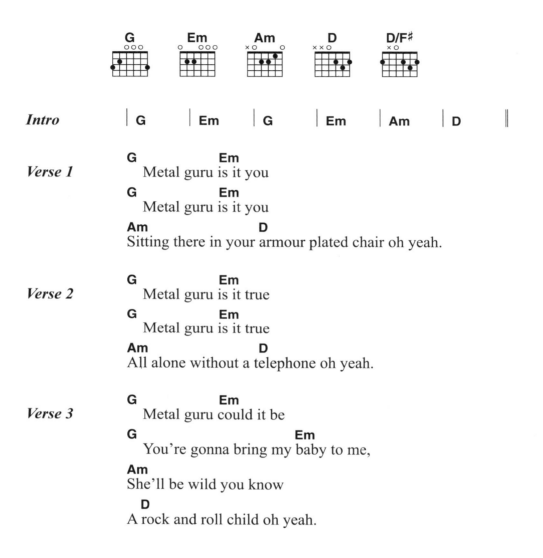

Intro | G | Em | G | Em | Am | D ‖

Verse 1

       G   **Em**
Metal guru is it you
       G   **Em**
Metal guru is it you
Am   **D**
Sitting there in your armour plated chair oh yeah.

Verse 2

       G   **Em**
Metal guru is it true
       G   **Em**
Metal guru is it true
Am   **D**
All alone without a telephone oh yeah.

Verse 3

       G   **Em**
Metal guru could it be
       G   **Em**
You're gonna bring my baby to me,
Am
She'll be wild you know
   D
A rock and roll child oh yeah.

Verse 4

```
G            Em
Metal guru has it been
G                        Em
Just like a silver-studded sabre-tooth dream,
Am
I'll be clean you know
 D
A washing machine oh yeah.
G            Em
Metal guru is it you
G            Em
Metal guru is it you?
```

Bridge

| G Am | D/F♯ Em | G Am | D/F♯ Em | Am | D |

Verse 5

As Verse 3

Verse 6

```
G            Em
Metal guru is it you
G            Em
Metal guru is it you
Am                    D
All alone without a telephone oh.
```

Verse 7

As Verse 3

Outro

```
    G            Em              G
‖: Metal guru is it you (yeah yeah yeah)
                Em
Metal guru is it you (yeah yeah yeah) :‖ Repeat to fade
```

No More Heroes

Words & Music by
Hugh Cornwell, Jean-Jacques Burnel, David Greenfield & Jet Black

Gm   C   F   B♭   Am

Intro ‖: Gm   C | Gm   F | Gm   C | Gm   F :‖

Verse 1

           Gm   C   F   Gm   C   F   Gm
Whatever happened to   Leon Trotsky?

                    C   F   Gm   C   F   Gm
He got an ice pick   that made his ears burn.

                  C   F   Gm   C   F   Gm
Whatever happened to   dear old Lenny,

                  C   F   Gm   C   F   Gm
The great Elmyra   and Sancho Panza?

Chorus 1

B♭   C   Gm
   Whatever happened to the heroes?

B♭   C   Gm
   Whatever happened to the heroes?

Verse 2

           Gm   C   F   Gm   C   F   Gm
Whatever happened to   all the heroes?

                  C   F   Gm
All the Shakespearoes?

                               C   F   Gm
They watched their Rome burn.

Chorus 2

B♭   C   Gm
   Whatever happened to the heroes?

B♭   C   Gm
   Whatever happened to the heroes?

Bridge 1

Gm   C   Gm   F
No more heroes any   more,

Gm   C   Gm   F
No more heroes any   more.

Guitar solo ‖: Gm Am │ B♭ C :‖: Gm Am │ B♭ Am :‖

‖: Gm Am │ B♭ F :‖: Gm C │ Gm F :‖

Keyboard solo ‖: B♭ │ C │ B♭ │ C :‖ *Play 5 times*

│ Gm C │ Gm F │ Gm C │ Gm F ‖

Verse 3

              Gm   C F Gm   C F Gm
Whatever happened to   all of the heroes?

                          C   F Gm
All the Shakespearoes?

                                         C F Gm
They watched their Rome burn.

Chorus 3

B♭   C   Gm
  Whatever happened to the heroes?

B♭   C   Gm
  Whatever happened to the heroes?

Bridge 2

Gm   C   Gm F
No more heroes any   more,

Gm   C   Gm F
No more heroes any   more,

Gm   C   Gm F
No more heroes any   more,

Gm   C   Gm F
No more heroes any   more.

Coda ‖: Gm │ Gm │ Gm │ Gm :‖ *Play 3 times*

No Particular Place To Go

Words & Music by
Chuck Berry

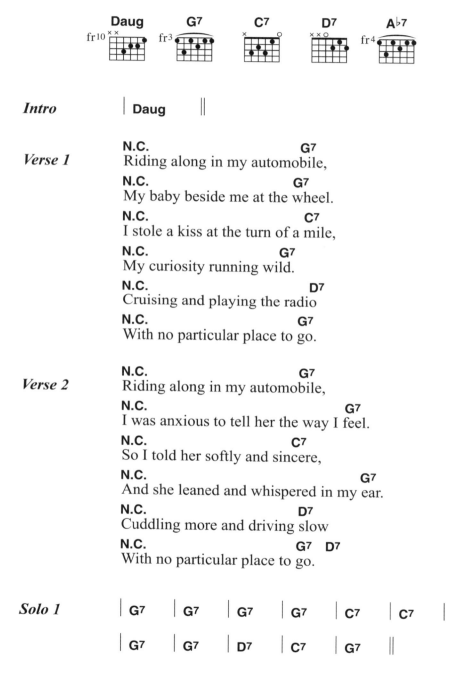

Intro | Daug ||

Verse 1

N.C.   G7
Riding along in my automobile,

N.C.   G7
My baby beside me at the wheel.

N.C.   C7
I stole a kiss at the turn of a mile,

N.C.   G7
My curiosity running wild.

N.C.   D7
Cruising and playing the radio

N.C.   G7
With no particular place to go.

Verse 2

N.C.   G7
Riding along in my automobile,

N.C.   G7
I was anxious to tell her the way I feel.

N.C.   C7
So I told her softly and sincere,

N.C.   G7
And she leaned and whispered in my ear.

N.C.   D7
Cuddling more and driving slow

N.C.   G7   D7
With no particular place to go.

Solo 1 | G7 | G7 | G7 | G7 | C7 | C7 |

| G7 | G7 | D7 | C7 | G7 ||

Verse 3

G   N.C.   **G⁷**
    No particular place to go,

N.C.   **G⁷**
So we parked way out on the kokomo.

N.C.   **C⁷**
The night was young and the moon was gold

N.C.   **G⁷**
So we both decided to take a stroll.

N.C.   **D⁷**
Can you imagine the way I felt?

N.C.   **G⁷**
I couldn't unfasten her safety belt.

Verse 4

N.C.   **G⁷**
Riding along in my calaboose,

N.C.   **G⁷**
Still trying to get her belt unloose.

N.C.   **C⁷**
All the way home I held a grudge

N.C.   **G⁷**
But the safety belt it wouldn't budge.

N.C.   **D⁷**
Cruising and playing the radio

N.C.   **G⁷**
With no particular place to go.

Solo 2

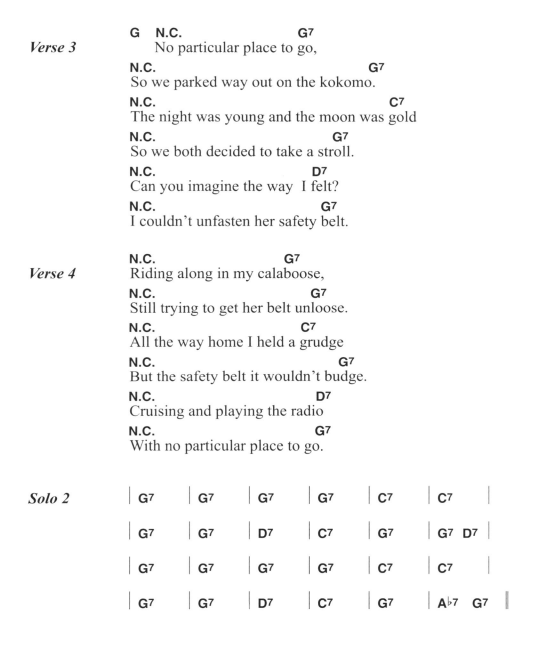

G⁷	G⁷	G⁷	G⁷	C⁷	C⁷
G⁷	G⁷	D⁷	C⁷	G⁷	G⁷ D⁷
G⁷	G⁷	G⁷	G⁷	C⁷	C⁷
G⁷	G⁷	D⁷	C⁷	G⁷	A♭⁷ G⁷

Pretty Vacant

Words & Music by
Steve Jones, Johnny Rotten, Paul Cook & Glen Matlock

A5   G   D   E   C

Intro   ‖: A5 | A5 | A5 | A5 :‖ *Play 10 times*

Verse 1

          A5   G
There's no point in asking,
        D   A5
You'll get no reply,
    G   E
Oh just remember, I don't decide.
    A5   G   D   A5
I got no reason, it's all too much,
    G   E   A5
You'll always find us out to lunch!

Chorus 1

       D   C
Oh we're so pretty, oh so pretty,
A5
   We're vacant.
       D   C
Oh we're so pretty, oh so pretty,
A5
   a - vacant.

Verse 2

       A5   G
Don't ask us to attend,
        D   A5
'Cause we're not all there,
    G   E
Oh don't pretend 'cause I don't care.
    A5   G   D   A5
I don't believe in illusions, 'cause too much is real.
    G   E
So stop your cheap comment,
           A5
'Cause we know what we feel.

Chorus 2

      D   C
Oh we're so pretty, oh so pretty,

A5
  We're vacant.

       D   C
Oh we're so pretty, oh so pretty,

A5
  a - vacant.

       D   C
Oh we're so pretty, oh so pretty,

A5   G E N.C.   A5
Ah, but now,   and we don't care.

Verse 3

           A5   G
There's no point in asking,

           D   A
You'll get no reply,

    G   E
Oh just remember I don't decide.

  A5   G   D   A5
I got no reason it's all too much,

        G   E   A5
You'll always find me out to lunch!

We're out to lunch.

Chorus 3   As Chorus 2

Outro

A5
We're pretty, a - pretty vacant,

We're pretty, a - pretty vacant,

We're pretty, a - pretty vacant,

We're pretty, a - pretty vacant,

And we don't care!

Should I Stay Or Should I Go

Words & Music by
Joe Strummer & Mick Jones

D   G   F   A   A⁷

Intro | D G | D N.C. | D G | D N.C. | D G | D | D G ||

Verse 1

    D N.C.   D G D
    Darling you got to let me know:

N.C.   D G D
Should I stay or should I go?

N.C.   G F G
If you say that you are mine

N.C.   D G D
I'll be here 'til the end of time.

N.C.   A A⁷
So you got to let me know:

N.C.   D G D
Should I stay or should I go?

Verse 2

N.C.   D G D
It's always tease, tease, tease;

N.C.   D G D
You're happy when I'm on my knees.

N.C.   G F G
One day is fine, the next is black,

N.C.   D G D
So if you want me off your back,

N.C.   A A⁷
Well, come on and let me know:

N.C.   D G D
Should I stay or should I go?

Chorus 1

N.C.   D   G D
Should I stay or should I go now?

                               G D
Should I stay or should I go now?

                      G   F G
If I go there will be trouble,

                              D   G   D
cont.   And if I stay it will be double.
                              A   D G | D   ‖
               So come on and let me know.

               N.C.   D   G   D
Verse 3   This indecision's bugging me   (esta undecision me molesta);
               N.C.   D   G   D
               If you don't want me, set me free (si no me quieres, librame).
               N.C.   G   F   G
               Exactly who am I'm supposed to be?   (Digame que tengo ser).
               N.C.   D
               Don't you know which clothes even fit me?

                        G   D
               (¿Saves que robas me queurda?)
               N.C.   A   A⁷
               Come on and let me know__ (me tienes que desir)
               N.C.   D   G   D
               Should I cool it or should I blow? (¿Me debo ir o quedarme?)

Instrumental | D   G | D   N.C.| D   G | D   N.C.| G   F | G   N.C.|

                | D   G | D   N.C.| A | A⁷ | D   G | D   N.C.‖

               N.C.   D   G   D
Chorus 2   Should I stay or should I go now? (¿Yo me frio o lo sophlo?)
                                        D   G   D
               Should I stay or should I go now? (¿Yo me frio o lo sophlo?)
                                  G   F   G
               If I go there will be trouble (si me voy va ver peligro),
                                  D   G   D
               And if I stay it will be double (si me quedo es doble).
                                  A
               So you gotta let me know (me tienes que decir):
                                       D   G   D
               Should I cool it or should I blow? (¿Yo me frio o lo sophlo?)

                                             G   D
Chorus 3   Should I stay or should I go now? (¿Yo me frio o lo sophlo?)
                                  G   F   G
               If I go there will be trouble (si me voy va ver peligro),
                                  D   G   D
               And if I stay it will be double (si me quedo es doble).
                                  A
               So you gotta let me know (me tienes que decir):
                        G   D
               Should I stay or should I go?

Strange Brew

Words & Music by
Eric Clapton, Felix Pappalardi & Gail Collins

Intro

| A | A | A | A |

| D9 | D9 | A | A |

E7♯9   D7♯9   A
Strange brew, killin' what's inside of you.

Verse 1

  A   D9
She's a witch of trouble in electric blue,

          A   D9
In her own mad mind she's in love with you, with you.

                 A
Now what you gonna do?

E7♯9   D7♯9   A
Strange brew, killin' what's inside of you.

Verse 2

  A   D9
She's some kind of demon messin' in the glue,

          A   D9
If you don't watch out it'll stick to you, to you.

                 A
What kind of fool are you?

E7♯9   D7♯9   A
Strange brew, killin' what's inside of you.

Solo

| A | A | A | A |

| D9 | D9 | A | A |

| E7♯9 | D7♯9 | A | A |

Verse 3

A   **D9**
On a boat in the middle of a raging sea

           A   **D9**
She would make a scene for it all to be ignored.

                       A
And wouldn't you be bored?

E7♯9   **D7♯9**   **A**
Strange brew, killin' what's inside of you.

Coda

A   **D9**
Strange brew,

A
Strange brew.

D9   **D7♯9**
Strange brew,

A
Strange brew,

E7♯9   **D7♯9**   **A9**
Strange brew, killin' what's inside of you.

The Passenger

Words by Iggy Pop
Music by Ricky Gardiner

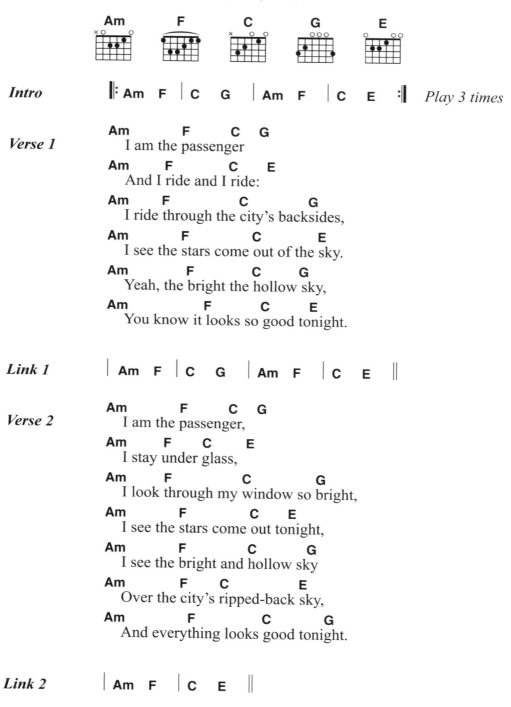

Intro

‖: Am F | C G | Am F | C E :‖ *Play 3 times*

Verse 1

Am   F   C   G
I am the passenger
Am   F   C   E
And I ride and I ride:
Am   F   C   G
I ride through the city's backsides,
Am   F   C   E
I see the stars come out of the sky.
Am   F   C   G
Yeah, the bright the hollow sky,
Am   F   C   E
You know it looks so good tonight.

Link 1

| Am F | C G | Am F | C E ‖

Verse 2

Am   F   C   G
I am the passenger,
Am   F   C   E
I stay under glass,
Am   F   C   G
I look through my window so bright,
Am   F   C   E
I see the stars come out tonight,
Am   F   C   G
I see the bright and hollow sky
Am   F   C   E
Over the city's ripped-back sky,
Am   F   C   G
And everything looks good tonight.

Link 2

| Am F | C E ‖

Chorus 1

```
        Am   F     C       G   Am   F    C         E
Singing la la, la la, la-la-la-la,  la la, la la, la-la-la-la,
Am   F     C       G
La la, la la, la-la-la-la, la la (la.)
```

Link 3

```
| Am   F | C   E | Am   F | C   G ||
la.
```

Verse 3

```
Am   F      C    G
  Get into the car,
Am            F       C    E
  We'll be the passenger:
Am           F          C      G
  We'll ride through the city tonight,
Am           F      C         E
  We'll see the city's ripped backsides,
Am           F          C      G
  We'll see the bright and hollow sky,
Am           F          C    E
  We'll see the stars that shine so bright,
Am   F       C    G
  Stars made for us tonight.
```

Link 4

```
| Am   F | C   E | Am   F | C   G | Am   F | C   E ||
```

Verse 4

```
Am          F      C  G Am   F        C      E
  Oh, the passenger      how, how he rides.
Am          F      C  G Am  F          C      E
  Oh, the passenger       he rides and he rides.
Am           F          C      G
  He looks through his window,
Am     F       C    E
  What does he see?
Am           F          C      G
  He sees the bright and hollow sky,
Am           F          C    E
  He sees the stars come out tonight,
Am            F      C      G
  He sees the city's ripped backsides,
Am           F      C      E
  He sees the winding ocean drive.
Am           F          C      G
  And everything was made for you and me,
Am     F       C      E
  All of it was made for you and me,
```

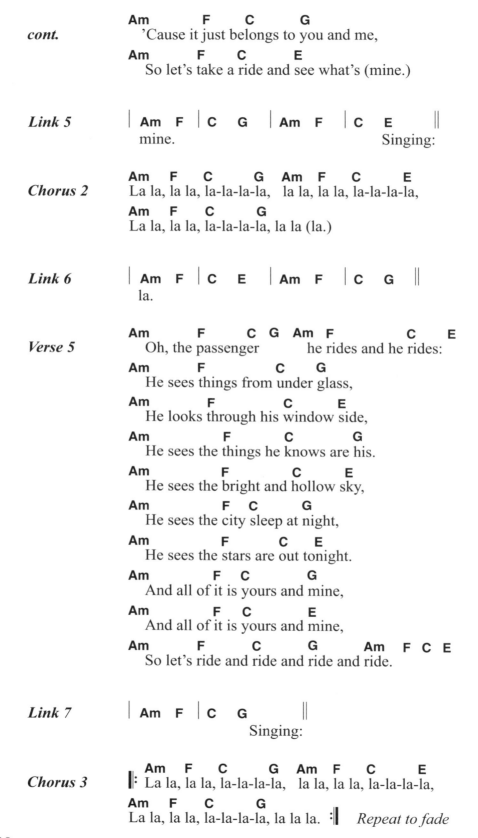

cont.

```
      Am       F    C    G
      'Cause it just belongs to you and me,
      Am       F    C       E
      So let's take a ride and see what's (mine.)
```

Link 5

```
| Am  F | C  G | Am  F | C  E     ‖
  mine.                     Singing:
```

Chorus 2

```
Am  F   C    G  Am  F   C       E
La la, la la, la-la-la-la,  la la, la la, la-la-la-la,
Am  F   C    G
La la, la la, la-la-la-la, la la (la.)
```

Link 6

```
| Am  F | C  E | Am  F | C  G   ‖
  la.
```

Verse 5

```
Am         F      C  G  Am  F            C     E
   Oh, the passenger      he rides and he rides:
Am       F         C    G
   He sees things from under glass,
Am        F          C        E
   He looks through his window side,
Am          F        C         G
   He sees the things he knows are his.
Am          F           C       E
   He sees the bright and hollow sky,
Am           F  C       G
   He sees the city sleep at night,
Am           F        C    E
   He sees the stars are out tonight.
Am          F   C        G
   And all of it is yours and mine,
Am          F   C        E
   And all of it is yours and mine,
Am        F        C       G        Am   F  C  E
   So let's ride and ride and ride and ride.
```

Link 7

```
| Am  F | C  G        ‖
              Singing:
```

Chorus 3

```
   Am  F   C    G  Am  F   C       E
‖: La la, la la, la-la-la-la,  la la, la la, la-la-la-la,
Am  F   C    G
La la, la la, la-la-la-la, la la la. :‖  Repeat to fade
```

Stupid Girl

Words & Music by
Shirley Manson, Steve Marker, Butch Vig & Duke Erikson

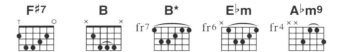

Intro

| N.C. | N.C. | N.C. | N.C. |

| F♯7 | B | F♯7 | B |

| F♯7 | B | F♯7 | B |

Verse 1

F♯7   B
  You pretend you're high,

F♯7   B
  You pretend you're bored,

F♯7   B
  You pretend you're anything

F♯7   B
  Just to be a - dored.

       F♯7
And what you need,

B   F♯7 B*
  Is what you get.

Pre-chorus 1

E♭m   A♭m9
Don't believe in fear,

E♭m   A♭m9
Don't believe in faith,

E♭m   A♭m9
Don't believe in anything

E♭m   B
That you can't break.

Chorus 1

F♯7   B
You stupid girl,

F♯7   B
You stupid girl,

F♯7   B
All you had you wasted,

F♯7   B
All you had you wasted.

Instrumental 1 | F♯7 | B | F♯7 | B |

                | F♯7 | B | F♯7 | B   ‖

Verse 2

F♯7   B
What drives you on

F♯7   B
Can drive you mad,

  F♯7   B
A million lies to sell yourself

F♯7   B
Is all you ever had.

Pre-chorus 2

E♭m   A♭m9
Don't believe in love,

E♭m   A♭m9
Don't believe in hate,

E♭m   A♭m9
Don't believe in anything

E♭m   B*
That you can't waste.

Chorus 2

F#7   B
You stupid girl,

F#7   B
You stupid girl,

F#7   B
Can't believe you fake it

F#7   B
Can't believe you fake it.

Instrumental 2 As Instrumental 1

Guitar solo As Instrumental 1

Pre-chorus 3

E♭m   A♭m9
Don't believe in fear,

E♭m   A♭m9
Don't believe in pain

E♭m   A♭m9
Don't believe in anyone

E♭m   B*
That you can't tame.

Chorus 3 As Chorus 1

Chorus 4 As Chorus 2

Chorus 5 As Chorus 2

Outro | F#7 | B | F#7 | B |

     | F#7 | B | F#7 | B ‖ F#7
                   You stupid girl.

Sultans Of Swing

Words & Music by
Mark Knopfler

Dm   C   B♭   A   F

Intro

‖: Dm | Dm | Dm | Dm :‖

Verse 1

            Dm
You get a shiver in the dark
     C   **B♭**   **A**
It's raining in the park but meantime
Dm   **C**   **B♭**   **A**
     South of the river you stop and you hold everything
F   **C**
     A band is blowing Dixie double four time
B♭   **Dm**   **B♭**   **C**
     You feel alright when you hear that music ring

Verse 2

         Dm   **C**   **B♭**   **A**
You step inside but you don't see too many faces
Dm   **C**   **B♭**   **A**
     Coming in out of the rain to hear the jazz go down
F   **C**
     Competition in other places
B♭   **Dm**   **B♭**
     But the horns they're blowing that sound
C   **B♭**   **C**   **Dm**   **C B♭ C**
     Way on downsouth   way on downsouth London town

Link 1

| Dm   C | B♭ | C | C ‖

Verse 3

          Dm   **C B♭**   **A**
You check out Guitar George   he knows   all the chords
Dm   **C**   **B♭**   **A**
     Mind he's strictly rhythm he doesn't want to make it cry or sing
F   **C**
     And an old guitar is all he can afford
B♭   **Dm**   **B♭ C**
     When he gets up under the lights to play his thing

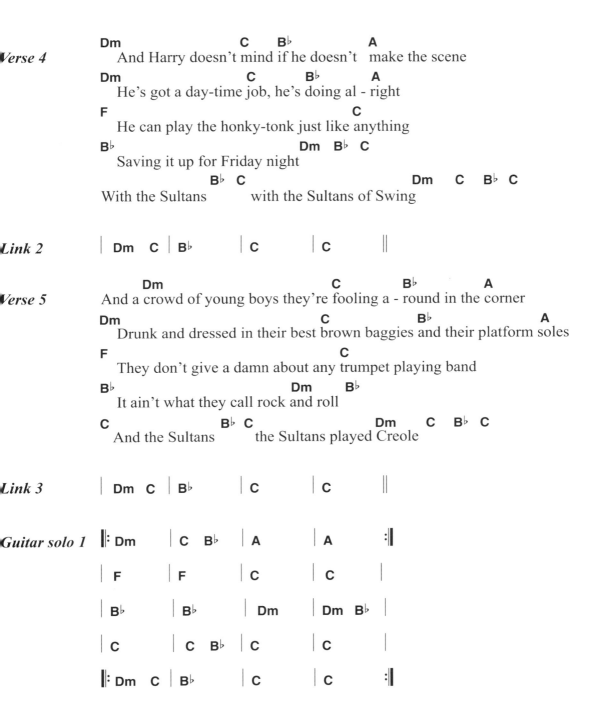

Verse 4

Dm   C   B♭   A
    And Harry doesn't mind if he doesn't make the scene

Dm   C   B♭   A
    He's got a day-time job, he's doing al - right

F   C
    He can play the honky-tonk just like anything

B♭   Dm   B♭   C
    Saving it up for Friday night

                    B♭   C   Dm   C   B♭   C
With the Sultans   with the Sultans of Swing

Link 2 | Dm   C | B♭ | C | C ||

Verse 5

       Dm   C   B♭   A
And a crowd of young boys they're fooling a - round in the corner

Dm   C   B♭   A
    Drunk and dressed in their best brown baggies and their platform soles

F   C
    They don't give a damn about any trumpet playing band

B♭   Dm   B♭
    It ain't what they call rock and roll

C   B♭   C   Dm   C   B♭   C
    And the Sultans   the Sultans played Creole

Link 3 | Dm   C | B♭ | C | C ||

Guitar solo 1   ‖: Dm | C   B♭ | A | A   :‖

                 | F | F | C | C |

                 | B♭ | B♭ | Dm | Dm   B♭ |

                 | C | C   B♭ | C | C |

                 ‖: Dm   C | B♭ | C | C   :‖

Verse 6

```
        Dm                        C          Bb       A
        And then the man he steps right up to the microphone
        Dm              C              Bb       A
        And says at last just as the time bell rings
        F                              C
        'Thank you goodnight, now it's time to go home'
        Bb                                   Dm      Bb
        And he makes fast with one more thing
        C                         Bb  C                       Dm  C  Bb  C
        'We are the Sultans       we are the Sultans of Swing'
```

Link 4 | Dm C | Bb | C | C   ‖

Guitar solo 2 ‖: Dm C | Bb | C | C   :‖ *Play 8 times to fade*

Sweet Home Alabama

Words & Music by
Ronnie Van Zant, Ed King & Gary Rossington

Tune guitar slightly flat

Intro ‖: D Cadd9 | G :‖ *Play 4 times*

Verse 1
D   Cadd9   G
Big wheels keep on turning
D   Cadd9   G
Carry me home to see my kin
D   Cadd9   G
Singing songs about the Southland
D   Cadd9   G
I miss Alabama once again

And I think its a sin, yes.

Link ‖: D C | G :‖

Verse 2
D   Cadd9   G
Well I heard mister Young sing about her,
D   Cadd9   G
Well, I heard ol' Neil put her down
D   Cadd9   G
Well, I hope Neil Young will remember
D   Cadd9   G
A Southern man don't need him around anyhow.

Chorus 1
D   C   G   C
Sweet home Alabama
D   C   G   C
Where the skies are so blue,
D   C   G   C
Sweet Home Alabama
D   C   G F C
Lord, I'm coming home to you.

Instrumental ‖: D   C | G   :‖

	D Cadd9 G F C
Verse 3	In Birmingham they love the gov'nor, (ooh, ooh, ooh)

D   Cadd9   G
Now we all did what we could do

D   Cadd9   G
Now Watergate does not bother me

D   Cadd9   G
Does your conscience bother you?

Tell the truth.

	D C G C
Chorus 2	Sweet home Alabama

D   C   G   C
Where the skies are so blue

D   C   G   C
Sweet Home Alabama

D   C   G
Lord, I'm coming home to you

Here I come, Alabama.

Instrumental ‖: D   C | G   :‖   *Play 10 times*

	D Cadd9 G
Verse 4	Now Muscle Shoals has got the Swampers

D   Cadd9   G
And they've been known to pick a song or two (yes they do),

D   Cadd9   G
Lord they get me off so much

D   Cadd9   G
They pick me up when I'm feeling blue

Now how about you?

Chorus 3

D   C   G   C
Sweet home Alabama

D   C   G   C
Where the skies are so blue

D   C   G   C
Sweet Home Alabama

D   C   G   F   C
Lord, I'm coming home to you.

Chorus 4

D   C   G   C
Sweet home Alabama (oh sweet home baby)

D   C   G   C
Where the skies are so blue (and the guv'nor's true)

D   C   G   C
Sweet Home Alabama (Lordy)

D   C   G
Lord, I'm coming home to you.

Outro

‖: D   C | G   :‖   *Repeat to fade*

Yeah, yeah Montgomery's got the answer.

Relative Tuning

The guitar can be tuned with the aid of pitch pipes or dedicated electronic guitar tuners which are available through your local music dealer. If you do not have a tuning device, you can use relative tuning. Estimate the pitch of the 6th string as near as possible to E or at least a comfortable pitch (not too high, as you might break other strings in tuning up). Then, while checking the various positions on the diagram, place a finger from your left hand on the:

5th fret of the E or 6th string and **tune the open A** (or 5th string) to the note (A)

5th fret of the A or 5th string and **tune the open D** (or 4th string) to the note (D)

5th fret of the D or 4th string and **tune the open G** (or 3rd string) to the note (G)

4th fret of the G or 3rd string and **tune the open B** (or 2nd string) to the note (B)

5th fret of the B or 2nd string and **tune the open E** (or 1st string) to the note (E)

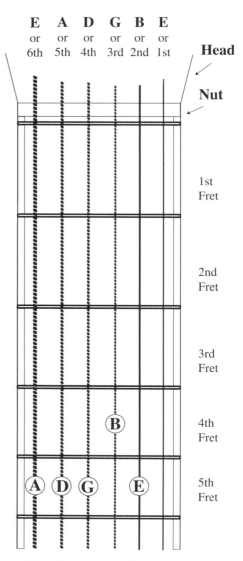

Reading Chord Boxes

Chord boxes are diagrams of the guitar neck viewed head upwards, face on as illustrated. The top horizontal line is the nut, unless a higher fret number is indicated, the others are the frets.

The vertical lines are the strings, starting from E (or 6th) on the left to E (or 1st) on the right.

The black dots indicate where to place your fingers.

Strings marked with an O are played open, not fretted. Strings marked with an X should not be played.

The curved bracket indicates a 'barre' - hold down the strings under the bracket with your first finger, using your other fingers to fret the remaining notes.

N.C. = No Chord.

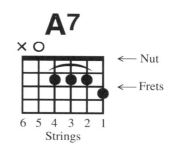

48